BOXING
THE COMPASS

Boxing
the Compass

RICHARD GREENE

SIGNAL EDITIONS IS AN IMPRINT OF VÉHICULE PRESS

Published with the generous assistance of The Canada Council for the
Arts and the Book Publishing Industry Development Program of the
Department of Canadian Heritage.

SIGNAL EDITIONS EDITOR: CARMINE STARNINO

Cover design: David Drummond
Photo of author: Linda Kooluris Dobbs
Set in Filosofia and Minion by Simon Garamond
Printed by Marquis Book Printing Inc.

LIBRARY AND ARCHIVES CANADA CATALOGUING IN PUBLICATION
Greene, Richard, 1961-
Boxing the compass / Richard Greene.
Poems.
ISBN: 978-1-55065-259-8
I . Title.

PS8563.R41747B69 2009   C811'.54   C2009-903488-3

Published by Véhicule Press, Montréal, Québec, Canada
www.vehiculepress.com

Distribution in Canada by LitDistCo
orders@litdistco.ca

Distributed in the U.S. by Independent Publishers Group
www.ipgbook.com

Printed in Canada on 100% post-consumer recycled paper.

In memory of
Richard Joseph Greene, Q.C., M.H.A.
1924-2007

Contents

ACKNOWLEDGEMENTS 10

PART ONE

On Sherbourne Street 15
At the College 16
Beside the Funeral Home 17
Rigor Mortis 18
Heroic Measures 19
Apparitions 20
Church Music Considered 22
The Living 23

PART TWO

Window 29
1000X 30
Oil-Barrel 31
Independence 32
Utopia 33
Custom 35
Two Chronicles 36
St. Ignace 39
Martin Royackers 40
House and Barn 41

PART THREE

Whaler 45
The White Fleet 47
Palliative Care 51
Crossing the Straits 53
Boxing the Compass 55

PART FOUR

Over the Border
I.   Amtrak and Greyhound 63
II. Austin 75
III. The District of Columbia: 2004 85

NOTES 97

Acknowledgements

I am grateful to the editors of *Oxford University Poetry Society Broadsheet*, *The Antigonish Review, Poetry Canada Review* and *Tickleace*, in which journals some of these poems were first published, as well as to the editors of the following anthologies: *The Practice of Spirit,* ed. Susan McCaslin (Toronto: St. Thomas Poetry Series, 2002); *Coastlines: The Poetry of Atlantic Canada,* eds. Anne Compton, Laurence Hutchman, Ross Leckie, and Robin McGrath (Fredericton: Goose Lane Editions, 2002); *The Backyards of Heaven: An Anthology of Contemporary Poetry from Ireland and Newfoundland & Labrador,* eds. Stephanie McKenzie and John Ennis (Corner Brook, 2003); *The New Canon: An Anthology of Canadian Poetry*, ed. Carmine Starnino (Mont- real: Signal Books, 2004). Some poems have appeared in my collections, *Republic of Solitude* (St. John's: Breakwater, 1994) and *Crossing the Straits* (Toronto: St. Thomas Poetry Series, 2004). Since this volume selects from work written over more than twenty years, the list of those who have offered shrewd and helpful criticism is long: the late Peter Levi, the late Sheldon Zitner, Philip Gardner, Mary Dalton, Barry Dempster, David Kent, Margo Swiss, John Reibetanz, A. F. Moritz, Kildare Dobbs, Jeffery Donaldson, Maureen Scott Harris, Leif Vaage, Allan Briesmaster, Colin Carberry, Marianne Marusic, Nicholas Swarbrick, Pavel Chichikov, Deirdre Greene and members of the Victoria College Writers Group. Linda Kooluris Dobbs has kindly provided the author photograph. I am extremely grateful to Simon Dardick and his associates at Vehicule Press for lavishing care on the production of this book. My greatest debt is to my editor Carmine Starnino: his selection from my poems is more insightful than any I could have produced.

PART ONE

On Sherbourne Street

I am at home in a high-rise
where at night the voice of being human
is a siren blare or a drunk crying fuck
something or other on Sherbourne Street.
Where I live we make our own danger
and the earth is hardly implicated
in our calamities: the man who tumbles
more storeys than he has years,
and the girls on Isabella who are dying
each night in the arms of Corydon.
Security men wear Kevlar vests
and follow a German Shepherd on a chain
through the hallways of my building.
The old sisters next door recall
when this was a desirable address:
the doorman wore a kind of livery then
and helped with parcels.
In St. James Town, the Carribean gangs
and the Filipinos watch one other,
skirmish, speak of war that may come.
My friend says I am mistaken
in thinking this place affordable.
But I say there is witness amid decay:
the street blossoms
in placards and buttons to save
the hospital from budget cuts,
and the church refurbishes
Mary and Bernadette in their grotto
for worshippers who pass at morning
and touch the stone.

At the College

Serpentine, the path unwinds its innocence
from building to building in flickering shade
where my students feed lazy raccoons muffins

and glazed doughnuts, as if to domesticate
the last wild things on this suburban campus,
though nothing can make the few deer unafraid

of engines, words, footfalls, the human rumpus,
or subdue the fox's wily nonchalance
and teach him not to kill anything helpless.

Here, among these fierce and sentimental students,
I stand on the edge of a world not my own,
snatching small goods from the large irrelevance

of what we do, making the old sorrows known
to children bearing their first calamities,
teaching solitudes to the newly alone,

explaining writers' exile to refugees
and notions of intrinsic worth to half-fledged
bankers, already driving smart Mercedes.

Yet they live by their hope, curiously pledged
to some afterness that will reward and bless
them for gifts that nature leaves unacknowledged

or earnest labours I grade at B or less;
they know some need of love that poets speak to,
and few can absent their hearts from every class,

however many dronings they may sleep through;
they will mark a perfect image or a phrase
and hear it years from now, wilder then and new.

Beside the Funeral Home

Twice a month, I watch special delivery
of modish coffins for customers anxious
not to be caught dead in the ordinary

or to neglect the last public decencies
and thus send parent, aunt or cousin abroad
again with no mark of comfort or success.

The undertaker's under-men gravely load
each empty coffin onto a folding cart
and then walk it from the alley to be stowed

behind a show-room where any broken heart
costs twelve grand and death looks like a Pontiac,
chrome-detailed and rust-proofed in every part.

But once cigarettes are stubbed on the sidewalk
and a monk in saffron robe has struck the gong
the cortège is led out by the Cadillac.

Cars reach slowly into traffic and are gone,
a sad departure for these new arrivals,
from a funeral home that calls itself "Wing On."

Rigor Mortis

"Rigor mortis is just the married man's
erection," opined one newly single,
in his cups, half-heartedly cynical,
to a table that cheered the performance.

How odd it is to quibble with a quip
when years have passed and wiseacre himself
will not remember what leapt from his mouth
nor any mock-shocked girl who lapped it up.

His own changed life has proved the saying false:
coupled again and in some kind of bliss,
his whole world rises with each hungry kiss—
not bad for a guy with a steady pulse.

Heroic Measures

In memory of Sheldon Zitner (1924-2005)

My fabled New Yorker,
you saw me off with advice on marriage,
"Keep it flying."
And with mischief turned to an older friend,
"I go to prepare a place for you."

That was after surgery, in the "Step Down Unit,"
your small body nested among the wires,
a screen to your left counting heart-beats,
and on your forehead a cloth to cool you.

None of this was really survivable,
but I supposed that you were not killable,
and that you and death would keep waiting for the blink.

    ∼

I bought a bottle of wine while you were dying;
it was somewhere on the Avenue of the Americas,
and from my change five folded ones

fell out of my pocket into the wind,
and in the dark five figures, one on a bicycle,
chased them down

and laid them in my hand:
so much, I thought, for the myth of the nasty New Yorker—
but what is sentiment in Manhattan?

Far from your bed and bones,
I heard you, still yourself, touching this milk
of kindness with your tongue:
"Repeat the experiment. This time, use twenties!"

Apparitions

It is the Feast of Our Lady of Lourdes;
this parish church, named for her, is crowded
as though it were Easter or Christmas Eve.
Once white as Rosedale, the congregation
is Filipino, Tamil, Carribean,
their Canada a few acres of shabby
towers across the street, the most densely
populated place on the continent.
Even the white men here are outsiders,
not husbands and fathers, but gay couples
who live in the streets just east of Yonge,
that other estrangement in the city's core.
The back of the bulletin advertises:
"Catholic Cemeteries," a pawn-broker,
"Alleluia Driving School—You're in Safe Hands!"
psychotherapy, two lawyers, a doctor,
and, always, firms providing "Remittances
To Manila", for mothers to send home
the scant harvest of minimum wage
to babes who know them as a photograph
or a voice down the telephone wire.
        I wonder at their fervour, the worshippers
of Mary, their stories of miracles,
healings, locutions, apparitions,
souls released from purgatory by prayers
to her, devotions "never known to fail."
The Tamils leave cookies beside statues,
and at the grotto, candles, money, toys,
in December, a coat for the shoulders of
Bernadette, lest she shiver in the light.
There is only a little extravagance
between this and my grandmother's yearly
pilgrimage to Ste Anne de Beaupré
or my mother's daily Rosary

and roll-call of the dead who, she believes,
will feel the betrayal in her own death
when no one prays for them.
     My feast is elsewhere
but not separate: my son's seventh birthday,
the third I have missed in as many years.
We celebrated with a phone call,
not long because his party was going on;
it was time to open gifts, and his friends
were there.
   My pang is less in this company,
their accents rippling the surface of hymns
that pour from childhood: "Immaculate Mary,
your praises we sing, you reign now in heaven
with Jesus our King...." The Rosary booms
from speakers wrapped in plastic, the Joyful
Mysteries counted off, as the crowd
circles the church in a slow procession
to pray at the Grotto. Rain falls steadily
and umbrellas blossom under street-lights,
as each of us holds a taper in wet hands.
I see in these faces a flickering grace
and glimpse my son wishing on his day's candles.

Church Music Considered

1.

The most popular piece of church music nowadays is "Error and Variations."

2.

In the more inclusive choirs, pitch is optional.

3.

This is the first choir that I have heard for which the fitting accompaniment is indeed the Hammond Organ.

4.

Percussion — like lumber falling from a truck.

5.

If one singer had found the pitch they would have had nine-part harmony.

6

A choir director on Good Friday: "I haven't been this nervous since my wedding, and we all know how well that turned out."

7.

This is just another nail in the cacophony.

8.

My noisy bass among a dozen sopranos—like parallel parking a bull-dozer.

9.

If prayer is the breath of a song, why so much karaoke?

The Living

In memory of Peter Levi , 1931-2000

I

One lifetime keeping the roof-beams and slates up
over how many lifetimes of Common Prayer
and Sarum Rite? Underfoot, manorial
dust of those who owned village and shire;
in the Chapel some pious barbarian
stretched out with his blade and bride,
retelling for a thousand years in stone
tales of Saladin and Christ's Sepulchre.
The windows make anthology of lives
given to small mercies and steady trade:
Zacchaeus called out of the tree by bequest
of an attorney; the coiling dragon
and St. George sacred to the memory
of a colonial brigadier; Mary
Magdalene breaks perfume on holy feet
remembering a cornfactor's widow;
in the churchyard, lives less prosperous
grow illegible under rain and moss.
Curate or curator, the priest among stones
serves the dead parish more than the living.

II

It was a thing that I almost wanted—
priest of the Church of England, as I had
failed to become one in the Church of Rome.
This was to be the unturning of paths
that turned. No longer "ours" but my own,
and yet bound by that imagined self
I could neither inhabit nor escape.
In the damp and cold of December
I sat by the small fire in a chaplain's

rooms, and wept for something in myself
that now I cannot name. It was desire
or it was mourning. It was, I think,
the shadow of a hill thrown forward
onto level ground, the illusion of ascent.

III

   He sent me to the Bishop, whom I could
not call "Milord," and then to a Canon
who thought me suspect because foreign,
and challenged me: "Why should you be ordained
and a woman not?" I bought approval
when I said, "I honour martyrs but wish
they had lived." It was sufficient, after all,
and he would have backed me, but without
enthusiasm— though what he did not hear
in me I heard, a way with mysteries
all too practiced, too polished, and too glib.

IV

   After two years, I tried it all again,
and I took my oath before a new Bishop
to live as an Anglican—a ritual
out of a ring-binder, coyly phrased
so not to repudiate old loyalties
or to offend against ecumenism—
this at St. Mary the Virgin, under
Newman's pulpit, and before the chancel
where they tried Henry's Bishops over bread
and sent them to the flames in Cornmarket Street.
And yet in that church, the best of witnesses
were the unremarkable living—the casual
vicar, who noticed me confused
on my first Easter night, handed me a bell
and nudged me when the moment came to ring.

V

Often, week-day Evensong at Christ Church,
the boy-angels lifting the Psalms with voices
that rose towards vaulted shadows and glass,
and the clergyman listening to his hand
for the true note a tuning fork made.
On a pillar opposite my usual pew,
the empty eye of a tiny carved skull
held my own and pulled me back from Purcell's
heaven with ordained thoughts of what was gone,
who had sung and listened, who had vanished
from this place in its thousand years of chanting.
But against all that weight of memory
I set the cold afternoon in Tom Quad:
staring into Mercury Pool, my daughter
leaned forward and fell among the fat carp.
Instantly, I snatched her from the water
and saw running towards us a black gown
and a flapping bath towel — a theologian,
fifteen years later to be Archbishop
of Canterbury, on his way to do a kindness.

VI

I saw him staggering in a lane beside
the Bodleian, the finest poet
I will ever know, lost in a place where
he had spent half his life. "Peter," I called.
He knew my voice and answered without looking
towards me. "Richard," he said, " I have
gone blind, temporarily, from eyestrain.
I need to buy shoelaces in the Turl.
Walk with me." I brought him to the shop
and left him there, though he seemed surprised
that I would desert him at a bad moment.
I had somewhere to go, an appointment
with the curate who was my counselor—
we were talking our way towards vocation.

So I left Peter there groping along
in the quest for shoelaces, yet remember
nothing else of that day but the poet
standing in a doorway. I did not see him
again. The day changed nothing, of course,
but it tells me how the ambition
ended. Soon, my prayer soured and I could think
only of death, something in myself
that I turned from, another calling that
certainty would kill. I made my excuses,
problems of finance and citizenship,
and closed the book on the matter of England.

PART TWO

Window

A window gathered light from the sky
and argued for life in a bad time,
as amid gesticulating boughs
of a stripped maple, its crooked fingers
raised in bitter emphasis,
an unseen orator spoke in mime.
The wind exhaled October like a threat
and stirred the leaves to riot
that merely loitered in their discontent.
The house itself leaked spirit
through the roof and walls,
received the cold airs passively,
those deputations bearing
seasonal warrants of arrest,
but the heart,
not ready to renounce its true estate,
saw the sky framed like a constitution
where the window gathered light.

1000X

The profusion of the microscope:
I live with my wife and child
among uncatalogued species of pleasure
that swim past like sudden tadpoles.
I can find no scale for the lesser miracles,
a domestic existence
whose landscapes are a table-top,
a bed-sheet and a sink,
whose horizons are paint and plaster,
and whose constellations
are filaments minutely hung.
Love is a conversation in a water-drop.

Oil-Barrel

Leaves enclose the mind
where love unclothes itself,
learns nakedness for the months of cold.
The wind fills with newspapers
and the leaves fall:
the year ends in whitened dark
wandering barefoot under street-lamps.
Deep drifts gather and migrate
across the last pages of the calendar;
cars vanish under a falling sky.
At morning love stirs
a little comforted by daylight,
shakes the night's snow from its limbs,
sees an unbearable light
refracted in icicles.
The snow-blower feeds on deciduous light
and trucks carry the morning away
in huge loads;
hour by hour, the light is less.
The mind trudges in its bitter wind,
following gaunt trees along a boulevard
where their shadows fell.
The spirit lives only in numbness now,
at finger-tips where death is beginning:
the oil-barrel breathes flame
in an implacable dark.

Independence

The edge of all the world,
an island, huge and empty,
swimming in fog, worn away
by currents warm and cold,
and the memory of glaciers
stripping soil from stone,
oppression which preceded history.
Torn from North Africa
floating through its million years
of independence, always at sea,
and the mystery of its inhabitants
before the Beothucks, Brendan,
or the Vikings,
before empire or dominion,
the republic of its solitude.
To study politics in the stone,
those hills which were volcanic,
the wrinkling and subsidence
of an ageing land,
the palm tree becoming pine,
and still the wandering.

Utopia

I

An immense acreage of solitude.
No one has lived here
or left more than a shadow
among shrubs and stones.
The hill falls to water
and a carious rock:
geology is a study of the spirit,
one place forming another
in the migrations of a continent.
I am always here
on a hillside of quartz and juniper,
a ridge over water
where the whales blow and dive,
and the grounded ice-bergs topple
in a smoke of gulls.
This place is twenty years of me,
the stark coastland of a question.

II

Who dares learn such emptiness,
contending with thoughts of ocean,
or interiors yet a wilderness?
And learning, who dares forget?
The world is more populous than the soul:
there are hermits in Soho.
Europe will have a radioactive Summer
and tumours subsequently.
This morning as I prayed
Americans flew past in a transport plane
perhaps too full of bombs for greeting.
I listen to my breath

and the machine that eats motor-cars
For breakfast;
they find nutrition in our old manoeuvres.
I am still listening to my breath,
I think that I am here.

III (Isaiah 22: 16-18)

What right have you here,
and what relatives have you here
for you to hew yourself
a tomb in this place?
See, Yahweh hurls you down,
down with a single throw;
then with a strong grip he grips you
and winds you up into a ball
and hurls you into an immense country.
There you will die.

IV

O my immense country of no place,
there is nowhere as strange as now.
I am alone in this acreage of breath,
landscape of spruce, fir, clover, and rock,
a lifetime expiring somewhere worlds away.

Custom

The world is drifting further from this world
and every hope is inwardly compelled
from nervousness and acts compounding noise
to strange exclusions and darkening surprise.

I imbibe new silence with every breath
and my range of purpose grows less and less
for clear beyond the customs of this heart
my life is drifting endlessly apart.

Two Chronicles

I

Gaius Writes

On the second day of the first fortnight of Xanthicus,
seven days before the calends of March
two hours after midday on the greater Sabbath,
when the ruling monarch was Jesus Christ,
in a year we think was 155,
Polycarp, the ancient father of Smyrna,
friend in his youth to John the Apostle,
refused the good advice of a governor
to swear by the luck of Caesar and thrive.

There were others,
some so scourged that their organs, their deepest veins and arteries,
were exposed to the eye and still they bore up.
This was proof they were not present in their opened flesh.
One named Germanicus spurred the beasts to feed on him
and roused the circus crowd to bitterness;
to punish bravery with another death,
they called for Polycarp.

Hidden away in farms, he prayed for the churches,
while the hunt drew closer.
He dreamed of his pillow in flames and ash
and knew then he would be burned.

"Eighty and six years have I served Him, and He has done me no wrong,"
his answer to the governor,
and tied to a wood-pile he gave thanks for what he had come to.

The fire took the shape of a hollow chamber,
like a ship's sail when the wind fills it;

it made a wall around the martyr's figure;
and there he was in the centre,
not like a human being in flames but like a loaf baking in an oven,
or like a gold ingot being refined in the furnace.

And when, at last, he did not burn, the confector,
finisher of wounded beasts and men,
opened him with a knife, cut into the aviary of his flesh
from which a single dove flew.

He was the twelfth to meet a martyr's death in Smyrna,
and what I glean of him is from his disciple Irenaeus,
the one who said, "The Glory of God is man fully alive";
he saw these things and reverently preserved the bones.

II

The Copyist
c. 250

"I, Pionius, have made a fresh copy of those writings in the hand of Gaius.
I found them after Polycarp the blessed revealed their whereabouts in a
    vision,
as I will explain hereafter.
Time had reduced them almost to tatters, but I gathered them
in the hope that the Lord Jesus Christ might likewise gather me."

Pionius entertained the Holy Woman Sabina and Asclepiades
on the anniversary of the martyrdom, knowing they were all to be seized.
He wove fetters for their necks, so that no one would think
they went freely to make the sacrifice and to taste forbidden meats.

Polemon the temple verger led them without other restraint
through the double gates of the forum
to the voting urns and the tribune's steps,
and there asked them to make the sacrifice.
The three refused all civil blandishments, every chance of life,
and Pionius spoke to the crowd:

"You men who boast of the beauty of Smyrna, who live by the river
    Meles,
and who say you glory in Homer,
remember that he said it is not a holy thing to gloat
over those who are to die."
And to Polemon:
"You have been ordered either to persuade us or to punish us.
You are not persuading us."

But Polemon, constrained by the fasces, had no authority to kill them.
Two weeks in jail they waited for the proconsul,
who put the question to Pionius,
finger-nails torn: "Why do you rush towards death?"
"I am rushing towards life."

He was nailed to the gibbet in the amphitheatre
with another named Metrodorus.
When the circle of logs burned and smoke filled his lungs
he coughed out his spirit.

Such was the innocent, blameless and incorruptible life
which blessed Pionius brought to an end with his mind fixed on
    Father and Son.
After his victory in the great combat,
he passed through the narrow gate into the broad, great light.
Indeed, his crown was made manifest through his body,
for after the fire was out, those of us who were there
saw his body like that of an athlete in the full array of his powers,
his hair lay in order on his head, his beard full as in its first
    blossoming.

St. Ignace

Though maps rendered the unknown as nothing,
this place, already made human by blood,
was made more so by an uncertain good:
the theatre of agonies playing
out in ritual hurt and holy dying,
contest of sacraments in the deep wood;
warrior and warrior-saint pursued
their separate glories in this clearing.

For the absent victors, pelt and powder
were the sanctity of Georgian Bay
and no ritual lingered among trees;
whoever died might yet be called martyr
for what that was worth at bourse or quaie,
far from the land they knew as vacancies.

II

Was it athleticism in dying,
the runner outrunning his nature's pain,
exercise of mastery and disdain
for flesh that hung estranged and burning?
No one goes from the self in suffering,
for torture stops time, this now again
and again, no movement that might sustain
the mind with a heaven of its ending.

Pain for pain, one place became another,
and the Calvary of their devotion
was an agony elsewhere yet the same,
their heart's gaze fixed upon Christ their brother,
who inhabited their silent passion
and the body of that moment in flame.

Martin Royackers

Young farmer, anointed with oils, hands laid on and priested,
never quite my friend though his spell tugged me
and held me at arm's length as I held him.

A head full of books at nineteen,
his conversation was hogs,
their cleanliness, their intelligence,
and the slanders against them.

He would hang his leg over the arm of a chair,
sit half a day with a book in one hand
and a never-extinguished cigarette in the other:
he once told a dozen celibates that reading was sexual
but disappointing when the pages ran out.

Student, teacher, editor, he was a scatterer of papers,
his words covered floors through twenty years and three countries.

Too much mastered by his jokes, he made himself solitary
until he found "his people" in Jamaica,
a ragged priest, farm-hand among farm-hands.

All this, of course, by report: I lost him long ago,
though the years seem an eyelid closed and opened:
the boy with his book and his cigarette
and the man on the verandah,
his blood scattered about him like ash.

House and Barn

One night a weight of snow would bring the roof
into the house, onto the empty beds,
and the walls would lean in toward sleep,
the bowed timbers snore in their collapse.

And there was weather enough to do it,
the snow burning above the black water,
the ocean blown onto the island cliffs
the seabirds sleeping on the back of storms.

Some nights a sudden wind wanted the barn,
and laid its hands on the rotten boards
to dance seduction back and forth till dawn,
whispering away resistance to the fall.

I looked through a window into miles of fog,
wondering when that world would break
and I not know what weather passed for dreams
in a bed where my first years grew cold.

PART THREE

Whaler

Great-grandfather,
        whaler out of Nantucket,
the harder sort
        who threw the harpoon,
        drew warm blood,
made huge death on the open sea.

Came home one year
        to find his land fenced
for ecclesiastical uses,
        tore it all down,
told the priest to go to hell,
        and would do his own praying
           after that.

Sailed till his knees went stiff
        with beri-beri
on a ship stuck
        in Antarctic ice.

My father worshipped him,
        remembered his deft hands
that could "put an arsehole in a crackie"
        with a hammer and a handsaw.

        The old man signalled
his affections:
        crafty hard of hearing,
heard the boy's words,
        even took his daughter's orders
           when she called him "Sir!"

Grew old jigging cod
          on the southern shore,
then fell from a roof
          and lingered days to tell
                    his last stories,
empty his mouth of good oaths.

What I have of him
          is my father's reverence for
his silence,
          a sense that pain will kill you
if you speak of it.

The White Fleet

I

Barefoot, they played football beside their ships,
the fishermen of Portugal's White Fleet:
hard tackles on the planking and concrete,
and always foreign tongues shouting pleasure
in tones unmistakable to a boy
who watched old leather fly to makeshift
goals among the nets and ropes and barrows.
The ships, docked three abreast, filled the harbour
with a swaying thicket of masts and yards
and the white blaze of their clustered hulls.
I cannot imagine how it must have seemed
at night on the Banks, their city of lights
over black waters that teemed with cod
but in port they were magical enough
to paint the town with rough benevolence,
a giving of half their lives, year by year,
to the fishing grounds and this Irish place.

II

I am five or six, holding my father's hand,
looking onto the deck of a square-rigger,
one of the last that could have laboured
on the open sea, this fleet's centuries
salted and stacked in a shadowy hold,
a few men on deck, olive faces burned
dark by sealight: they stand for thousands.

III

Two lives, divided by sea and season,
some fathering casually in St. John's
children they might not speak of in Lisbon
when Autumn sailed them to their legal loves.
As for the rest, they were faithful or cheap,
fished abroad and bred quietly at home.
In a city of rum-drinkers, they drank
the wine that traveled with them, sold brandy
on the dock to the bootlegger women.
Public order bore with their offences,
and the constabulary made nothing
of loud drunkenness and small affrays,
because their charities stood in balance:
at any late hour, a Portuguese crew
would genially pour out their twenty pints
to save some stranger bleeding at St. Claire's.

IV

They rowed out, single men in their dories,
as the ship stood to seaward like a wall
built hard against the ocean's killing depth.
They paid out trawls, hooks baited with caplin
or squid, and hauled in the twisting cod
until their boats brimmed with silver thrashing.
Then pulling the oars back and back they brought
the dories to the ship, loaded their catch
in lowered tubs, and climbed out of the sea.
But sudden mists came on the Banks, white ships
vanished, and there was nothing to row for
but the fog-horn sounding on a muffled deck.
Easy enough to pass all safety by,
go in circles or row far past the ship
towards a swamping on the open sea.

V

Fishermen in procession from their ships
carry Our Lady of Fatima
up through the city's winding Old World streets
to the Basilica of the Baptist—
this to honour Mary in their other home
and to make a tighter kinship in her prayers
with those who got the gist of an Ave.
That was years before I was even born.
Their virgin stands now in a shrine beside
the altar, kindly and bland and southern
in the midst of a severe architecture,
out of place among terrible stone saints.
I look for the fishermen in their gift
and find that they are barely knowable:
their hands hardened by rope and oars and salt,
hers a little pale plaster outstretched;
their sailors' eyes narrowed by the sun,
hers widened toward the light's clemency.
And yet she, Stella Maris, was the prayer
they uttered when they left port in blessed ships,
the prayer for plenty, the prayer for passage.
Fish and fishers gone, she prays for them still,
their dangers passed and all petitions moot.

VI

Something ended: thirty years of dragnets
harrowed the seabed to a kind of hell.
I cannot remember when the last white ships
went through the Narrows, old friendships extinct,
and the ocean breeding only grievance.
At the far end of the harbour I watch
a container ship swallowing cargo,
and, before me, three or four fishing boats
roped to the wharf waiting for a good year.

So many lifetimes of the Portuguese
are berthed in the silence of this afternoon,
as their voices ring to a quietness
in memory, just at the moment's edge,
where sunlight reflects on moving water
a bounty beyond our best intentions.

Palliative Care

The journey goes past healing to places
like this, where demerol and morphine
separate the last of our consciousness
from a body shrinking away to pain.
I nod to the man who sits on his bed
inhaling oxygen from the thin tube
under his nose, as if it were some vice;
he seems a corner-boy with cigarette,
spitting because it's manly not because
he must. I know his brother, the tenor
at the Basilica; when he visits,
I wonder how health and sickness can make
two versions of a single Irish face.
Further down, I discover Jim Wade,
a parcel of bones; I had supposed
despite the ship-wreck of his tumoured lungs
that he was well enough to live a year;
here among some books and canvases,
he shows me a paragraph of his on night
and sleep that kindly Boyd Chubbs has inked
in a strange and loving calligraphy.
By the weekend, he is in his coffin.

At the door of her bedroom, I see her
as she was in my childhood, on the arm
of a last boyfriend before she lost all
hope of marriage, or as in photographs
from the 40s when there were always Yanks
to dance with at the Base, but never one
to set against a mother's will that she
should stay at home and give up on men.
Ninety pounds of her barely dent the bed,
as she stirs from palliative twilight
to greet me with a mumbled affection.

My father's choice was not to tell her,
but I'm sure she knows by now that something
as bad as cancer is killing her.

The nurses are professionally kind;
I could not do the things they make routine,
the labours that accomplish less and less,
washing limbs and folding them when it's time. .
They adjust the drip beside her bed,
and record the increments of morphine
on a chart, as well as tranquillizers—
'It's for the anxiety.' But she rarely
wakes, and so they are medicating dreams,
one pill to take away the fear of death.

When she does wake and words come back to her,
she asks about the little dog she made obese
with chocolate treats, mentions the mother
who became her only spouse and widowed her
three years before, or she asks for 'Richard,'
meaning my father, who gives her answers,
understands things better than anyone.
But tonight she startles me by asking,
'Rick, what is going to happen to me?'
I cannot face her pain and tell a truth
or play the counselor and make her say
of what she is afraid, and so I lie,
'You will be okay, you will be okay.'

Soon she does not wake, though perhaps she hears
the priest's ritual, and knows in her drowned
consciousness that breath is nothing now,
takes the last little swallows of air, and goes.

Crossing the Straits

The sea is moving under our passage,
an old year out and a new year in
between Port aux Basques and North Sydney.
The ship rolls in the first breaths of a gale;
it has been so long, ten or twelve years,
since I last sailed, I do not trust my legs
or stomach to hold against the weather,
so lie still as a narrow berth allows,
reminding myself that disaster
is a kind of lottery, and to sink
as hard as winning millions on dry land,
and that sailors, having made profession
of storms, know their work and die old.
In an hour, anxiety drowns in sleep;
the mind, as ever, opposes passage,
and I dream of my flat in Toronto,
its wooden deck stretching across the roof,
a ship remote from this night's turning.
At six I wake and walk through lounges
where some have sat up all night playing cards
or talking, their New Year's revels queasy
and circumspect where the ship's movement
began the hangovers before the drinks.
More have slept in the rows of La-Z-Boys
before an almost bloodshot T.V. screen,
its hoarse voice still croaking festively
about the crowds that gathered in Times Square.
The gales have subsided and the sea is calm
less than an hour out of North Sydney;
a heavy breakfast later, I walk along
a deck where snow-crusted lifeboats are hung.
I imagine that in summer this is
the ship's best place, but the air is frigid
this morning, and Newfoundlanders crossing

the Straits see water enough in warmer times
to forego the prospect now, but this moment
of pent chances, between home and home,
is not mine alone, and for most who travel
there is some tear in memory between
the longed for and the given, what they left
and what they are. Nova Scotia looms,
and the purser summons drivers to cars
in the ship's belly, where tractor-trailers
are already roaring for landfall.

Boxing the Compass

"Sailor's Word-Book, To Box the Compass. Not only to repeat the names of the thirty-two points in order and backwards, but also to be able to answer any and all questions respecting its division." (OED)

An ocean of small, sunken boats between here
and there, though you are going nowhere now
but as shifting tides and your lungs allow,
square-rigged or gaff-rigged with tubes of salt water
and gales out of a barrel, tame northeaster
to brace you against the harder winds that blow
you on to your beam ends and lay you low.
It is in you now this storm and this seawater.
So I wait with you in a crowded dark
where ageing men must revive or perish,
and wonder, my father, what under morphine
your dreams are? The old man on his ship's deck
and you a boy among the ropes and canvas—
that hour's sunlight over all the days you've seen.

           ~

Remember when you breathed so easily,
lit a pipe behind cupped hands when the wind blew?
Trees you planted bending every way from true,
grey water hove up as breakers out to sea,
baffling gales turned round in their weatherly
boxing of the compass, all thirty-two
points of tumult bearing on Baccalieu
or Bell Island? And things I could not see—
'Whales,' you said, 'Out there, dozens of whales.'
An hour later, we watched through streaming glass
but I could not tell a pothead from a wave.
Forty years on, I lie through a night of gales
in your emptied house and see them pass,
blow, plunge in waters deeper than a grave.

~

An old Land Rover grinds through uncut snow
and stops before a gate the latest storm
has shut—summer's lane-end to the farm
that reaches under boughs white-weighted low.
Seven or eight, I can't follow where you go,
'Just step into my track—you'll come to no harm.'
A boy's shape vanishes into the man's form,
tramping after you, my lifetime ago.
Tonight, and there will not be another,
you will go through the last of your gates
and snowdrifts—I will hold your cooling hands
and watch death like a change in the weather—
your throat closes and your body waits
as deeper whiteness gathers and extends.

~

Choosing between slums, you always said Queen's
Road, and never rounded the corner to
Allan Square and whatever else was true
of that blighted childhood, the hard scenes
of your fifth and sixth years—Greenes
and Mackeys (down the shore) shaken through—
boy-uncle, grandmother, infant sister too,
suddenly fevered and in their coffins.
And what about your brother's story
of the little plane at Christmas, a gift
withdrawn at Twelfth Night and given over
the next Christmas, and twice more? A drift
of black snow and coal smoke in Allan Square,
poverty winding back the tale of Magi.

～

She stitched, at nineteen, in the Reids' house,
seamstress to the magnates of narrow gauge,
remembered the Rolls Royce in her old age,
 and every button she sewed to a blouse.
Grew resolute, iron-handed with a spouse
whose sailor dullness held her like a cage;
her last child died and then the marriage—
had her affair and offered no excuse.
She fed you, clothed you, and taught you the grudge
against your father—she kept you devoted
all the years she lived. When I asked, you lied
and said he drowned at sea. It was the nudge
of years that led your clouding mind through it—
you asked me to find where he was buried.

～

Four years-old, you way-laid Brother O'Hehir,
begged him to let you begin your years of chalk
and ink wells; he sent you and your friends back
home with candy from his pocket, 'Next Year.'
So you took revenge on his ankle rubbers
left on the stairway for the muddy walks
to Mount St. Francis; hammer and roof tacks
pinned the principal to the top of his stairs.
That was tactics, of course, not strategy,
for there was no way he would let you in.
But in time, he lifted you out of the gutter
you were born to, gave you math, oratory,
Moore's Melodies, the creed, and church Latin—
and that now-expiring gift—a future.

~

"'There are old pilots and bold pilots
but no old, bold pilots'—words to live by,"
said survivors of Arras and Vimy
who took you up in creaking Tiger Moths
till you had your hours and, big in your boots,
headed for the air-shows; you looped high
for a wing-walker, and for ten bucks would fly
a Piper Cub through the hangar's gates.
But wings iced, you lost a Beaver's engine
over the Cabot Straits, and silence was
what death sounded like when it was most near.
The engine sparked at last—you came in
between flaming oil-drums on your only pass
over a snow-bound runway that taught you fear.

~

'Trusty and well-beloved', I think it says,
'Learned in the law', scroll signed by some hack,
Her majesty's man, a politician paid back.
Offered that job—pomp, circumstance, a place
to wither out your years with flabby grace,
drenched in vice regal brandy and dry sack—
you could not imagine white tie and hard tack,
ceremonial scissors and borrowed face.
You shrugged, and settled for no honour
higher than the silk, though some you aspired to
were offered and withdrawn. A declining decade
of shrinking fortunes brought you closer
to your final self—fearful of each clue
of illness, holes in memory, all things frayed.

~

'Sure, I can put an arsehole in a crackie' –
ancient brag that stops with you. I can't drive
a felt-nail straight home, let alone contrive
with glue and dowels some larger trophy
of uncontested manhood—mahogany
tables or that line of tight-knitted shelves,
relics of cunning, of a mind that thrives
on small perfections of geometry.
For your last battle, you chose carpentry
as Granda hefted handtools in your childhood.
Wits decaying, you measured twice, cut once.
So we guess at the merits of joinery,
close seams in maple, the grain of hardwood
hand-planed, spokeshaved, fit for endurance.

PART FOUR

Over the Border

I too had receiv'd identity by my body,
That I was I knew was of my body, and what I should be I knew I should
    be of my body.
        —Walt Whitman, 'Crossing Brooklyn Ferry'

Cold victualing I seized, I hoisted up
The old man my father upon my back,
In the smoke made by sea for a new world
Saving little——a mind imperishable
If time is, a love of past things tenuous
As the hesitation of receding love.
        —Allen Tate, 'Aeneas at Washington'

He is out of bounds now. He rejoices in man's lovely,
peculiar power to choose life and die —
when he leads his black soldiers to death,
he cannot bend his back.
        —Robert Lowell, 'For the Union Dead'

1. Amtrak and Greyhound.

I've decided to stay out of the clouds
and instead make my book on the ground,
go cheap for weeks in archives and look
for a great man's life in letters I've found,
trade my comfort for more time searching,
sleep in hellish hotels and avoid planes:
from Toronto to Boston to Austin,
this is a summer of buses and trains.
Lightning to start with, torrents in Oakville,
and on to Niagara where the rains
are redundant and the bus like a barrel
goes over the border into spectacular
air. Utica draws near, rain is less,
the hills shimmer behind hills, line by line, then
fade to white in the beauty of the mist,
but the bus can't take it — the top hatch
leaks and the grim-faced driver can't promise
a new bus at Rochester but he can try.

Evening brings me down by the Mass Pike
into Riverside, with knotted muscles
and my joints in mutiny. A cabbie
tells me he's not supposed to take young males
as some desperate boy has broken out
and alive or dead is going back to jail.
I am flattered to be thought a bandit
but soon he spots the white among my hair
and decides it's safe to take my money.
'Park Inn, Boylston Street,' I say to the mirror
that frames his eyes. A silence all the way
to Chestnut Hill — but at the door he asks,
'You know, don't you?' 'Know what?' 'About this place.'
'Someone killed here?' A smile breaks the mask
of caution, 'Don't think I should tell you, see,
you won't be happy.' And he won't be happy
till he tells — 'Well, this was the hotel where three
Arabs stayed before they went to Logan.
Up there in Room 432. And right here,
their boss Mohammed Atta parked his car.'

~

I suppose that ghosts are ordinary
and must resemble what they will not leave.
I look for the hints of insanity
that might linger where they must have prayed,
some breath of theirs still hanging in the air,
some weight of finger on a numbered button
just above the pasted notice that declares
this elevator is 'NON-COMPLIANT'
with a code that changes every year.
My room is haunted by tobacco,
the smell of bourbon, hash, and spilt beer.
The ghosts of old brawls are in the splintered

doors, cracks mended with screws and bolts.
What terror for some girl in the bathroom
when the wood broke through and a boot
cleared the way for a pimp's or client's fist?

But morning is saner and the hotel
belongs to the elderly and the sick
who need a doctor or a hospital
better than they have at home, and Boston
is the one chance to get rid of this thing.
Table by table in the breakfast room
the quiet talk is surgeons and healing:
partners of a lifetime refusing shade.

～

Here I am among quiet Americans:
my days in an archive—boxes of words
from Malaya, Vietnam, Paraguay –
where murder merited no records
beyond a writer's comment as he passed
on the way to some other death, a phrase
to catch the loss of everything and move on:
here the heart of the matter is the witness
of onion-skin and letterhead—boxes
of what he alone saw and spoke of once
in hurried letters only a typist touched,
all marked: 'Dictated and signed in absence.'

～

Boston South Station, a clustering
of kiosks selling bad food and good coffee.
A jeweler plies his trade among husbands
heading home to trouble in the country,
needing something now to appease the wife
for girl-friends, long hours, or his game of golf.

At noon, I board the Lakeshore Limited;
most seats are filled and I must wedge myself
in beside a sleeping man—belly broad
enough to cover the seat he hasn't bought.
The train is rolling and a steward remarks
that every seat is sold and we'll all be tight.
I spot blue sky through a rusted canopy
at Springfield after days of Boston grey.
Between Pittsfield and Albany
an eighteen-wheeler stands in a truckstop,
its side painted: 'Mobile Chapel: Transport
For Christ'—some odd apostle of the pikes
offering chapter and verse for comfort
to lonely men who live by benzedrine.
Then farm country, tractors parked in fields,
small houses looking out from the forest
and the broad leaves holding light in their hands.
I get to know the man across the aisle –
born in Liverpool, lived then in Belfast,
now Colorado—he carries whisky
in a bag and every hour pours a glass.
A service stop at Albany and he
is gone to find a bar, says he has a map
with a pin for every place he's had a pint in.
He returns with another beer to sip
in his seat and I ask how he would mark that—
he considers and says he'd draw a line.
Evening comes and I walk to the café
car: 'No, sir, we are all out of wine.
There's Gin—no tonic—it's been that kind of day.'
At a table two women confide out loud
and a third listens: 'My mother and I
are both recently divorced and we are proud
to be out travelling.' 'I have a place
that costs half-nothing so I put what I got
on tickets to cities I want to see.'
The mother goes to the rest-room, leaves in thought

the daughter whose voice grows quieter:
'Mother just had a quadruple bypass—
so we are doing all our living now.'
Back to my seat and sleep does not come—
the hours watching darkened windows glow
through Ohio, where streetlamps gather
into crowds, then scatter to ones and twos,
with miles between them of wheat and corn
and farmer's solitude. I open my eyes
on mountains of coal—tangles of catwalks
and piping where the godlike chimneys thrust
themselves into filthy clouds; this is
Gary, chief city in the kingdom of rust.

~

In the Great Hall of Union Station,
under the Canal Street Doors, I sit
on a pew in a temple whose worship
is movement. All over the continent
stations from the twenties speak in marble
to the will of steam over distance.
Overhead small panes of glass bring down blue;
Minerva and owl, Persephone and rooster,
are carved in relief high on the wall,
and the stars and stripes hang like curtains—
patriotism at either end of the hall.

Commuter-less on Saturday, there's room
for a ghost—I see him suddenly go
past in the rush of 1944,
my father newly at home in Chicago,
twenty then, all before him —rising man
in the stockyard business of beef and pork —
in his private time, he is Tom Swift,
tubes and transmitters and airplane props;
even now, he speaks of cloud as 'ceiling'

and the best of days he calls 'unlimited.'
I see him brown-suited, clutching a Gladstone;
his eye on the future cannot see me
or see his world ending in a wheel-chair
and a walker and the dozen pills
and poisons of his eightieth year.

∾

A bow-tied beggar approaches me beside
the Sears Tower: 'Do not be alarmed,
I am a poet and I am intent
on spreading the word. No one will be harmed.
I would like to buy some poetry books
that cost fourteen dollars. I'd like to know,
sir, can you help?' I give him a dollar—
he asks for a second. 'I have to go.'

A hundred and fifty foot trail of blood
in large drops winds across a street and down
an alley. There is no way to follow
and no one to tell. I am a stranger in town.

∾

'Train 22 Annulled beyond St. Louis'
flash-flooding in Texas, a freight train
derailed, and I am holding a refund
and taxi-fare for the Greyhound station.
A dash with heavy bags and I stand
in line while the ticket sellers chat.
The bus to Memphis pulls away and I
am killing time—seven hours to wait.
A dank place, temple to nothing, poor men
and women carry clothes in pillow-cases.
A girl with a grip twice her age opens it
on the floor and carefully replaces

a pink T-Shirt folded with absolute
precision, then fastens the satin divider
and closes it up. Her boy-friend, two knobs
of metal in his chin, presses things tighter
into a canvas bag so he can jam
more clothing in. And all of it into
a locker then—to wait their hours out.
I bury my eyes in a book not wanting
acquaintance here as each adolescent shout
contains a naked threat of knife or gun.
Three hundred pounds of man sits down beside me—
his chest is thick and his shoulders three feet across;
he wears ragged sweat pants, a shirt too small,
feet in flip-flops—his knee is bouncing
and he wants my eye. Half an hour passes
and he gives up waiting—'Where you going?'
There is no choice but to talk and turn it around,
'Austin. How far are you going?' 'By morning,
I want to be in Omaha. I've been sick
in Florida and have to get to the medical
school for an angioplasty real soon.
I had a heart attack—been in hospital.'
How odd that I had judged this man a threat.
'But why take the Greyhound? What's that about?'
'Flying could kill me. Doctors won't let me try.
I haul beef from Omaha down south
to Jacksonville and then cornseed back.
Got this indigestion burning feeling.
Pulled to the shoulder—passed out in the truck.
The people from the scales come and got me
Or I'd of died there. They said it was the second
one I had—ignored the symptoms of one
ten days before. Left everything behind
in the rig, my wallet and my clothes.
Gave me this stuff when I was leaving,
enough to see me home. My wife faxed
a copy of my commercial driver's

license—it's all I have for I.D.
You can't travel if you can't prove who you are.'
He pulls up his shirt to show where the sensors
had been attached to his body. I ask,
'What was it like, cooped up for two weeks?'
'A lot of tests. Had to give a lot of blood.
I hated all the needles, the jabs and pricks.
One went in there.' He points to his groin.
'What's going to happen now to your career?'
'I'm finished, my heart couldn't take the strain.'
'That's awful.' 'Well no. I have a new little girl,
I have a house that's paid for. My father
has a business I can work for. Things could
be worse. I'm down now but I'll get better.'
I ask, 'Is it harder to drive a truck
or one of these?' He looks to the buses
parked outside the window and turns back,
'The bus, I think, because of the riffraff.
I worry now even in the restroom.'
He adds with odd intensity, 'You never know
who you are going to meet.' Strangers loom
like another threat of death to a body
suddenly undefended. 'Listen, I'm
thirty-six years old and I'm really scared.'
I look at my watch and know that it's time.
'I wish you all the best with this thing.
I hope that you have a perfect recovery.'
'I hope so too, if the good Lord wills it.'
Embarrassed, I say, 'That's a certainty.'

     ~

So many places I'll not go back to,
black rubber on asphalt carries me out
of my way, the wrong bus from Chicago
into Kentucky, sleepers riding south,
waking where they intended; a Greyhound
sign under a single bulb in some town

marks, after all that incognita, ground
you know, certainty in the stepping down.
Sarge, the last driver, gets on and blesses
all his drowsy passengers with Baptist
courtesy, and with a strange gentleness
bids them lie back in their seats and rest,
asks 'y'all be really quiet, I mean extra,
— this little baby here is just two days old.'

       ~

Sunrise in the station at Paducah
waiting out the slow hours of my mistake
till a bus through Memphis and Arkansas
lands me in Texas for the next day-break.
But for now the gaze of Dale Earnhardt, still
living, and life-size, on a coke machine
two years after he struck Daytona's wall—
I remark on the strangeness of the scene
to a man who misses irony, senses
sympathy instead, and opens the door
to a stranger as one who also mourns.
'Dale was a great man,' he mumurs, heart-sore,
and tells me then he's going to roof his
father's barn with corrugated sheets of steel,
'Hard work. I have a gift for it,' he says.
Then an old man, his limbs all spindles
plants his sore feet in a weary stretch,
complains of arthritis in every joint,
and begs a dollar on his way to church.

The Greyhound men confer and I am sent
with the clean light of morning on my face
to Memphis where young soldiers from Fort Hood
spend a little leave with Elvis at Grace-
land before loading their duffle bags
for Iraq. A white-haired veteran

with a Legion pin stands sad and quiet
while his wife mothers two infantrymen
in conversation, a corporal and a private,
gives herself as family in a moment's
acquaintance, cheerfulness and promised prayers,
a whole heart summoned for two boys,
sensing this is what her war owes to theirs.

~

And I am off again, past sunken fields
and swamps and meadows over-grown.
A drawling buzz-cut beside me opines
'That's the kind of land you buy on the phone.'
And after that, Arkansas—Little Rock
a city of towers where I had expected
poultry and poverty in Clinton country.
But Hope was a kind of sadness perfected,
roofs sagging with rot and bill-boards boasting
Bubba's birth-place and a water-melon
festival, and what you see in passing
tells you more about its favorite son
than a million words of anecdotes
or a lifetime spent channeling the news.

'Bill likes burgers better than anyone
in the county,' booms a voice set loose
from nearly private chat to a bigger
boasting – first names with the chief of men
—claims he ran the Denny's where the governor
wolfed down all the flesh he didn't press.
'Got to know him well.' The conversation
fades beyond a mumbled 'How about that?'
Then for an hour the grilling of a cook
in uniform. He wants to know what's what
with Army equipment—diameter
of a frying pan, depth of a soup pot,

the quantities of lard in a kitchen
where, he supposes, bad food could get you shot.
'And you ma'am, what takes you out on the road?'
'Oh, this and that.' And there it ought to have ended,
but he thought he had a secret by the throat
and squeezed more tightly than he intended.
'C'mon, Ma'am, I bet you have a story.'
'No.' He looks in her eye and both pull hard,
she towards silence, he to possession.
'Family things' she says measuring each word
she gives up to him. 'Yeah?' 'You don't want
to know.' 'Can't be that bad.' And twenty people
sitting two and two, five rows either way,
know she'll hurt him—at last he's pitiful.
'I go to see my son, he's in prison.'
Abashed, the big red face is human now,
Bursting with apologies for prying,
and she says it's fine but will not let him go.
She looks into dark at Texarkana,
'I see him once a month—it's the best place,
he's all I have. Drugs took my children.
He had two sisters and one killed herself
in a motel with sleeping pills and the other
couldn't bear to be without her, so drove
off a bridge, leaving just their brother.
I think that bars are all that keep him here.
He'd kill himself or court a killing,
and I just can't bury another one.'

Words exhausted, they fade to unwilling
friendship and the bus is quiet again.
Waco and Crawford and other histories
pass by in shadow. Into Dallas then
and the big men hurling our suitcases
from bus to bus, and nothing more certain
than that I will reach Austin with only
what is on my back and in my two hands.

On my last bus, I am in another country:
a man from county Sligo come to tell
the Texans about windmills; Quixote
backwards, he hopes expert hearts will swell
at his numbers and diagrams and start
the monsters spinning under every sky.
I am tired, but I think I have not dreamed him.
'At home, they won't even give this a try—
in Ireland wind is a wasted resource.'
He falls silent a little after I fall asleep.
An hour before sunrise I wake in Austin
to face the last consequence of traveling cheap:
No bags — learned opinion places them in
Tulsa: 'Be here tomorrow. Guaranteed.'

II. Austin

This is the 'Woo', a dorm named Goodall Wooten
on Guadalupe, the street they call 'The Drag.'
Once boys only, eternally rootin' tootin'—
beers poured from balconies onto the heads
of passers-by, and one famous resident
who'd slide down a pole in his boxer shorts;
now co-ed and substance free, but low-rent
still and half-empty out of term. I am old
in this company but can stretch my money
to a month among the manuscripts
if I can bear the noise of intimacy:
next door a couple makes hours of love
with a knocking sound and breaks the clinch
at 1 a.m. for post-coital video
whose wailing sound-track is Chinese.
But how few among these Texans are like
the yahoo and the red-neck we suppose them:
kids of intellect, whose casual talk
is subtle: two boys obsessed with tennis
wait for Wimbledon to start, and measure
champions: Sampras and Agassi,
Becker and Borg, Edberg and Laver:
'Don't talk to me about McEnroe,' says one.
'John McEnroe is something God did.'
And all of them cunning with computers
with odd fields of study, the woolly aphid,
the pancreas, a numbered gene, some star
you cannot see, a potentate in Siam—
a boy who wants to animate, an engineer
who will make bridges so light and cheap
that famine workers will carry them in trucks.
Of course, my room is ragged—two beds,
a knee-high fridge, a pair of narrow desks,
yellowing stucco and a ceiling fan.
My balcony overlooks a basketball
court, elevated on girders, with parking

underneath, beyond it an alley
where street people sleep among the trash cans.

~

A pay-phone at the 7-11
and I am back in touch. My daughter
in Frankfurt destined for the Ukraine,
she is fascinated but cannot bear
the smell of smoke constantly in her hair.
My step-mother numbers off the pills:
warfarin that I knew as a rat poison,
digoxyn, a beta-blocker, aricept,
a steroid for his lungs, but radiation
seems to have cleared his prostate,
so the latest news is only half-bad.
My amusing fiancé fears my travels
will get me put away as sick or mad
and of my work remarks, 'So you spend
your days reading other people's mail?'

~

A Gutenberg Bible and the first
photograph (bitumen of Judea
on pewter, eight hours exposed),
the desk of Edgar Allan Poe (don't touch),
a picture of Marilyn reading Ulysses
(doubtless striving for a shapely mind),
and the walls a kind of Parnassus,
after-life for poets and novelists
who sell their papers and their likenesses
into the keeping of the Texans.

~

'There's that ole rascal Rick Greene, one of our
re-peat customers' says Tom Best, under
his cowboy hat, first of old friends I see.
Then Pat Fox, photographer, designer
and amputee—she runs the Reading Room,
having quit the Pentagon after a mugging
in D.C. —'He struck my leg with a pipe
and wondered why I didn't fall. I kept tugging
on my bag and I wouldn't let it go
and he tugged and whacked till he was
bewildered by a leg that wouldn't break.
I left the city and the job because
of the risks — But I never thought a jet
would crash just in the spot where my desk was.'
Here too, I find Jim Watson, English prof
in a family of surgeons. His father
trepanned a dying Thomas Wolfe in 1938,
watched the fluid shoot three feet from a skull
packed with a 'myriad' of tubercles,
and then he faced Julia and her clan
who in madness could only pray and accuse
the doctors of killing a healthy man.
After work, Jim pours me Johnny Walker Red.
Tears hinted, he laments his father's going
and tells me Frost alone got it right:
'Just read "An Old Man's Winter Night."'

~

Pat Fox takes me out to the Hill Country,
but first we come to the double bill-board
for micro-surgical vasectomy
reversals — this on highway 290
outside the town of Dripping Springs.
On to Johnson City and the LBJ

ranch and birthplace—we board a little bus
where the presidential voice speaks loud
 and tells us that in Hill Country we're in
'a very special corner of God's
real estate.' And why not? A sparse heaven
of low hills, caves meandering in limestone,
juniper and shinnery oak rising
from thin soil beside the Colorado
and the Pedernales. We watch a film
on LBJ and the western White House,
a president hurtling about his own land
in a Lincoln, great sheets of splash
when he fords a brook at reckless speed.
You knew you mattered when he called you here
to watch his many televisions and inspect
his longhorns and his pricey Herefords.
He is buried, with all his distress,
in a family plot with a spot reserved
for Lady Bird, who in blind widowhood
has rescued the face of the Great State
with wildflowers that asphalt was killing:
antelope horn, baby blue eyes, turkey-foot,
knotty pondweed, zigzag iris,
big love nolina and kidneywood,
false garlic, false nightshade, false gromwell,
rabbit tobacco and barometer bush—
gracious additions to a legacy
of civil rights won and a long war lost.

       ～

Another day brings us to the town of Hunt
that stands a hundred miles from anywhere
on the mind's map, farther than quaintness
though it is quaint: the bank is a counter
in the general store and the restaurant
closes for meals. No, farther —in the land

of true oddness, where farmers reap
a kind of lunacy with a callused hand,
there is a man who took to raising
monuments in his meadow: cubes of wood
like long coffins stand in a wide circle,
some propped up, standing as a human would,
supporting others laid horizontal,
sprayed with concrete that would fool a druid
unless he came up close and knocked for
hollowness under the stone-faced plywood.
A hundred swallows nest in the high places
where coffin on coffin makes a corner,
and if anything can surprise me here,
it is their sudden flight, the three arrows
of beak and tail out of an aperture
in a nest of mud you didn't know was there.
Around the monument are faces,
all familiar, splayed noses that vanish
under a thick brow; three of them, twelve feet
high, serene where the hawks flourish.
It is Easter Island in a sea of grass.
In a pen across the lane alpacas
are lazily gazing on the things of Texas
and wondering who put them there.

∼

The *Dallas Morning News* tells of Bill Pickett,
the immortal cowboy who could wrestle
a steer with only his teeth. As a child
he watched the ranch dogs tugging steers, bulls,
calves and cows, and learned to bite the upper
lip, then twist it down, no sweat at all.
There he stands in the photograph, showman
with his hands in the air and his teeth clamped
on the steer's lip and the beast not knowing
what is coming next from this rodeo champ.

He made all the money he could handle
and then the Wild West Show went bust.
Will Rogers said everyone loved old Bill—
and that may have included animals,
except for the horse that kicked his skull,
which, sadly, was his last unbroken bone.

~

At the Renaissance market at 23rd
it is the summer of love again:
beads strung as they do it in Ecuador,
hemp necklaces, tie-dye, scented rocks,
lava lip gloss, magnetic bracelets,
horseshoe nail business card holders,
potpourri, candles, Guatemalan hats,
and the works of 'Fluteman Eric' in bamboo.
I walk in a forest of gray pony tails,
and marvel at their will to continue
in the creed of their youth: peace and free love
and Hendricks on guitar and Kent State
and Woodstock and My Lai and Chairman Mao.
These are the flowers of 1968.

~

At C.C.'s coffee shop on Austin's Drag,
a man sits with books and muddy papers
that he carries about in shopping bags.
On a table by the sidewalk he props
his ikons and translates, or says he does,
the psalms of David from ancient Hebrew.
He is a man of huge emphasis,
and says that the Palestinians must be
crushed, and as if it fell to him, insists,
'I don't like it, but they leave me no choice.'

My attention wanders from this war-like
scribe, and I look to the sniper's tower
and imagine Charles Whitman's bullets strike
up and down the Drag as they did in sixty-six.
Depression, rage, a tumour in his brain,
nothing accounts for his day of madness,
thirty-one wounded and fifteen slain;
I'd have thought him more sane than my psalmist,
marine, bank clerk, and an Eagle Scout—
I'd have missed the point, until I had seen
bodies, one with a bullet through his mouth.

       ~

I slip in to Mass at St Austin's Church
beside the dorm and hear a young priest
say that today is the feast of St. Norbert
who lived nine hundred years ago;
he turns to an aged concelebrant,
'Father Phil knew him well.' The old man glows
and the congregation convulses.
He says, 'Norbertines are an order
dedicated to pure liturgies
and when asked what they would die for
their answer will always be elegance.'
Laughter acts on the Lazarus will
and the sickness of the year is less,
but I think, 'Lord, the man you love is ill.'

       ~

I am in dispute with Austin's birds;
at morning, a starling fights me at Starbucks
for a pastry—wins a scrap from my hand
and I become this small bird's Daddy Warbucks.
I will feed a bluejay by the Ransom Center
because of loyalty to a baseball team.

But under the trees I confer with a scholar
who fears my work will trespass on his theme
and in the midst of diplomatic talk
a pigeon swoops down to bite my sandwich;
I throw him the crust and he withdraws to some
high bough and from his terrible vantage
discharges on the bald pate of the poor
professor who mops his scalp with a hanky
and goes off, still anxious and unsure.
At evening I eat at a taco stand
where a grackle lets out a cruel shriek
and flies at me like a Messerschmitt,
nakedness of apetite in its beak.
Another Mass, another priest, this one
from Japan, describes a peasant convert
who grasped Father and Son but of the third
asked, 'Who is this strange, honorable bird?'

~

Elsewhere I'd fill an evening with talk
but without work or love or television
I am compelled in Austin to walk
away the heaviness of shapeless time,
so face south towards the Colorado
River where the Congress Avenue Bridge
pours out into the first hint of shadow
a million and a half freetail bats
seeking their thirty thousand pounds
of bugs and flies each night to make fat
the nursing newborn 'pups' who must migrate
to Mexico in the fall. From gaps in
concrete and steel they shoot like twists
of black paper in a savage wind
or a billowing of ash, and they are gone
into the hunting ground of residential streets.

Most nights, I amble back by the Capitol,
its red arches and dome of granite
all vast, as if in 1888
they uttered its dimensions like a vow
or statement of purpose in a place
that seemed empty, ungoverned and remote.
On the grounds, the bones of memory:
tributes to the Alamo, firefighting volunteers,
the Texas Rangers and disabled vets,
the cowboys and the female pioneers.
And then the blinkered boasting for the dead—
a monument to confederate comrades
in what it calls 'The War Between the States.'

I see the poor men on Guadalupe:
one half naked by the Baptist Church
who sits cross-legged through the days of heat,
his skin exposed but still untouched
by a sun that is furious till dusk:
his legs and arms are thin but not like death
and his eyes are empty though intent –
I think of snake or grackle when I pass,
as pass I must. I see another man beside
the Wells-Fargo bank, probing its machine
with folded envelope, a search for money
in its lair. Then he forces a stick in—
to no avail—and he ends by shouting
against the steel and striking with his fist.
Another day, there is a chance to help:
I come upon a woman slipping fast
into a coma, her young husband stoned,
and I do the little that I may, call
for paramedics from a merchant's phone.
The poor are with you always when you walk.

~

I wake to good-byes. The files are closed
and put away — not a word more to type.
An hour left, I am in the grip of ghosts
and with a ten-dollar Kodak pursue
friends and strangers with a tearful snap.
I am troubled by a sense of something owed,
though bills are paid and no one's left to thank.
I climb aboard the train, my bags are stowed,
and I settle my limbs in the last seat
among the bodies headed north and east.

III. The District of Columbia: 2004

By train, you see the backs of things: yard, shed,
Buick that has not moved in years, mattress
on end and sodden beside a fence that sags,
its wire slack, and a dog guarding this refuse
because someone believes it is worth stealing.
Grimsby then Hamilton: spools of sheet metal
and mounds of muddy scrap, and Dofasco,
steel mill in an ocean of automobiles.
But suddenly I am out of steel
and into wine country —vines still bare
in April, hung on horizontal wires,
all waiting now for the first leaf and bud.
Bridge across the Niagara river:
white water to the left, to the right still green,
and at the border INS men work
the aisle: 'Where are you going?' they ask me;
'Washington, D.C.'
                    'Why?'
                            Question so quick
and simple you stutter like you are caught
in a felony – I ramble on about my book,
cut off at the lethal word 'archive,'
my dullness a sign of authenticity.
Behind me two middle-eastern men
are pressed, claim they live in Connecticut,
'What's the area code?' A moment's muddle,
the question comes back, 'The area code?'
No answer and then more things seem wrong.
They are led away down a platform
for harder questions and the train is gone.

    ~

An afternoon of fog and we are going slow.
Dusk begins at Amsterdam, where great houses
over-look the river, and the lit face

of a clock in Schenectady assures
me that I'll miss the next train to DC.
After mid-night I am standing in Penn
Station where they can discern
among the different kinds of traveler—
a glass corral to keep the vagrants out:
present your ticket and you may occupy
one seat whose fixed arm-rests forbid
sleep, so late travelers doze upright
necks twisted and heads falling to one side.
In an office with a blue lighted sign
portly Amtrak police smoke cigarettes
and emerge to move the beggars on,
the shufflers who root for something fit to eat
in garbage cans and the light-footed one
who waves two hands above his addled head.

~

At 7:30, I am in Washington
under the barrel-vaulted ceilings
of what used to be the largest station
in the world—of all Beaux Arts temples
to steam, this would be the Vatican,
built by a shanty-town named Swampoodle
on the banks of a creek called the Tiber,
and all of life contained here: ice-house,
Turkish baths, bowling alley, mortuary.
In 1953, a train rolled free, crushed
a newsstand, and broke the marble floor.
Air travel brought disuse, roof collapsing
and toadstools sprouting where Kings and Queens,
Presidents and even Roosevelt's corpse
had met with music and stiff salutes;
rescued by commerce, the concourse
is home now to Victoria's Secret,
The Body Shop, The Knot Shop that caters

to necks, an 'Afro-centric multi-
cultural art gallery' that specializes
in 'collectibles' and the 'one-of- a-kind',
four book stores, a cobbler, a shoe-polisher,
and two offices for the lost and found.

∾

The streets of Georgetown are out of time,
one ancient house of blue granite on M Street
was erected before tea and tax
turned colonies into musket-bearing states—
the oldest are stone and then came brick—
houses built at the edge of pavements,
fashionable, then slum, now revived as chic.
Parked cars proclaim their business in bold letters;
a van is marked: 'JOHN C. FLOOD Plumbing'
and then, lights flashing, 'GERM'S AMBULANCE.'
More apt naming brings me to the Lauinger's
'Gunlocke Room' where bits of paper are guarded
against trespass—I think of Kissinger's
remark: 'Academic fights are so
vicious because the stakes are so small.'
Piecemeal refusals—what I may and may not
read while someone else is free to read it all.
I spend days here, tongue bitten, typing
love letters from Graham to Catherine—
passion in Paris and Kikuyuland,
a dive-bombing, then drinks in Saigon,
and a paddle-boat along the Congo
among the human ruins of leprosy—
yearning, a taste for death, the will to know.

∾

'Why ya staying here?' Asks a cabbie
—to me, the taxi breed is kin to Yoda.

I have no answer—I got what I paid for:
cheap, remote and dangerous. 'I tell ya,
the hookers do 'em one after another
in these rooms.' That night, I am on the phone
to my fiancé when a knock comes.
No hello: 'I gotta get a bottle of wine.
You got wine? I gotta get wine.' I say no.
'You got wine? I gotta get a bottle of wine.'
No again and I close the door on her.
Saturday morning, the maid is cleaning my room;
I wait by the motel desk, reading the paper;
the manager, a sedate black man
with white hair stands behind security glass,
talks through six drill-holes made for speech.
A chevrolet pulls in by the door:
the driver shouts, 'You mother fucking bitch,'
leaves his car and runs in to the counter,
but the old man's hard to intimidate,
'Woman just called down that you are trying
to break into her room—you're not doing that.'
'I am here for Room 221, mother fucker.'
'She says you are trying to break in.'
'Mother fucker, that's lies, you mother fucker.'
'I am not your mother fucker. Your mother's
a ho, mother fucker.' 'Bitch, mother
fucker, bitch.' He squeals his tires on the way
out of the lot. A police cruiser
and a van pull up—for other business:
one corner of the lot is marked by police tape
'Do not cross.' Still, the sign says, 'No vacancies.'

~

Pavel is a poet and an old friend;
he regards my digs with courteous disbelief,
and hurries me off to the 'Holy Land in
America,' the intricate cells and hives

of worship at Mount St. Sepulchre,
run by the Franciscans in Brookland.
Its chapels and shrines are eclectic
renderings of sacred sites in Palestine:
Gethsemane is a valley of purple
tulips, roses, just-blooming azaleas.
There is a winding circuit of grottoes
that passes through Nazareth, the catacombs,
a crypt with the bones of St. Benignus,
the purgatory chapel, and back to Bethlehem.
Fifteen scenes are depicted in as many
chapels of the Rosary portico,
where an angel imparts the surprise
of his greeting in two hundred tongues.
On Good Friday the Friars carry Christ
lifeless on a pallet through a chamber
hung with oil-lamps to another where
on a stone shelf he waits for his rising.

Pavel lives a quieter life than he used to:
In 1991, an American
journalist in Moscow waiting for the putsch,
he kept the company of dissidents,
men and women who might die of speech
in a city of watchers and secret police.
He wrote on the poisoning of the White Sea
where fish were laced with dioxins
that were killing humans quietly.
He was handed papers for the eyes
of Gorbachev only, signed by the chief
of the KGB, confirming that public
health was a martyr to chemistry.
Izvestia's editors grew suddenly afraid:
'I was carrying not a newspaper article
but something like a typewritten, armed grenade.'
At the metro station in Pushkin Square
he knew there was no place he could go

where he might not be made to disappear.
He rode to Taganskaya and rose
on the long escalator praying all
the while: 'Lady, get me out of here.'
At the top, he heard a flautist playing
'Ave Maria' and he felt certain of her care,
and who's to argue with his certainty?
He lived to throw the hand-grenade, went home,
and in ten year's safety wrote a thousand poems.

      ~

From the second floor of a coffee shop
on M I look out onto a tray of petunias
hung like a collar round a streetlamp;
a day of blue skies has broken into
thunder and Georgetown's athletic girls
dash under cover, and everywhere
laughter as immense umbrellas unfurl.
Caught in the storm is a downed policeman,
leg broken where he tripped in a gutter;
the paramedics attend, brace the leg,
and lift him swearing on a stretcher.
A bus creeps by, and on its front rack
a single bright bicycle dripping rain.

      ~

Sunday morning: I head down North Capitol
where the First Amendment impedes my right
to be aimless. Three hundred thousand
with broom sticks to hold placards upright:
'Who Decides?' and 'This Is What a Feminist
Looks Like.' One T-Shirt reads 'MINE'
with a long black arrow pointing down.
At a Starbucks there are 56 in line,
at another, 30—cappuccinos

and lattes to fire change and to preserve
the right to choose. After speeches from
two Senators and from Whoopi Goldberg
who waves a coat-hanger, some slip away
to protest global trade and the IMF
in Foggy Bottom—a day of double outrage
for strong-voiced chanting soldiers of the left.

~

It was in Washington that I saw
my first Nazi—at Union Station
where I waited for a train with my father
in 1979—a conversation
I did not seek and could not end—a man
with floppy hat, dark glasses, moustache,
trying to look the part of secret agent,
rendered absurd by the tiny suitcase
he pulled behind him like a Pekinese—
told me straight he was a Nazi: 'Hitler
could have fixed Europe, given a chance.'
He said religion was the problem here:
'I collect photographs of churches
Burning—and every one of them should burn.'
I wonder what my father was thinking,
as I tried to escape this crazy talk:
he did not give any sign of listening,
but his body gathered to a tautness,
as if he might break this bastard's jaw
to get it shut. I can't remember how
I got free, but I remember he withdrew
suddenly and pulled his Pekinese away
to peddle dreams of white supremacy,
the Third Reich and the KKK
to people more respectful of the peace.
My father's war was spent in business—
tried to sign up underage, but the sergeant

had not counted on maternal rage, dismissed
the boy recruit as soon as shouted at,
and afterwards he flew the ocean once
delivering a DC-3 to North Africa,
but Hitler's war belonged to someone else.
The day of my 'Nazi' was the interval
between two trains that would get us
to my mother's relatives in Greenville.
We made our way through the Capitol;
I photographed my father on the steps,
gazing far and looking Senatorial.

⁓

The news from Newfoundland is almost good,
my father clear-headed and on his feet,
though age will not wind back nor the heart
muscle heal; he has reached a stalemate
with his death and must play again soon.
George, his simpleminded handyman,
was burning brush in an empty oil-barrel,
and left it smouldering behind the barn.
Something caught and long flames reached out
threatening grass-fire that would light the trees,
the barn and then the house. At sight of smoke
my father with a bucket hurried
there, made six more trips before it was out;
he seems delighted to have burnt his sleeve
though he says he feared a heart attack:
all this in the nature of a reprieve.

⁓

At 6:00 pm the cars are bumper
to bumper on Constitution Avenue;
horns rage as jets fly low into National.
Again, time is up, and I have seen too

little of a place. A bicycle path
takes me beside the reflecting pool
and then, at once, I come upon a granite
pavilion—with arches on its four sides,
the word 'Atlantic' carved in it.
Inside four eagles on tall pillars lift
a laurel; on the floor are inlaid dates.
I have read in The Washington Post
that the veterans are dying at a rate
of 1,100 per day—their beds a second
Normandy where patience alone
passes for a beach-head or a victory
among survivors of the sixteen million.
This place has been opened a month ahead
of dedication to steal a march on age
and sickness. Two tall fountains are ringed
by smaller ones, with seats along the edge
of an oval pool. Beyond that another
pavilion—for the Pacific War.
A wall of blue marks each hundred dead
in service with a single gold star.
Each state and territory is represented
as a column linked to those beside it
by a bronze rope: I think of how far
Wisconsin or Idaho must have seemed
when a sub foundered on the ocean floor
or a Mustang exploded in the air.
There are, perhaps, a thousand people in
the plaza, mostly the young and curious,
and only two or three who might be vets.
An old woman rests her varicose
legs beside me and stares a little upward
in the privacy of her sunglasses.

I make my way to Abe Lincoln's knee
where Gettysburg and the Second Inaugural
are cut letter by letter into the stone.

One sentence speaks grimly from the wall:
"Both parties deprecated war, but one
of them would make war rather than let
the nation survive, and the other would accept
war rather than let it perish, and the war came."
I sit outside at the top of the steps,
my back against a column; the sun
declines brightly behind the monument.
I notice then in the middle distance
the foot of the Washington Monument
wrapped, for safety, in a tall white fence,
and I can see no way of getting there.
I walk back along the reflecting pool,
where a family of ducks declares itself
sovereign over the National Mall,
mother and ten followers unbothered
by noise or by minutes of silence,
the click of cameras or the snap of flags.
They paddle crazily among remnants
of winter, the mud and the rotted leaves,
casually insisting on what comes next.

Notes

"The Living," pp. 23-26: Peter Levi was a prominent British poet, who left the Catholic priesthood for marriage; in his later years, diabetes caused him to go blind. Christ Church is the largest Oxford College and its chapel is actually a cathedral with a choir school; among the professors of divinity living at Christ Church in the 1980s was Dr. Rowan Williams, who became Archbishop of Canterbury in 2002. The University Church of St. Mary the Virgin was the site of the trials in 1555 of Latimer, Cranmer, and Ridley, bishops under Henry VIII accused of heresy by Mary I; in the nineteenth century, John Henry Newman served as vicar of St. Mary's before his conversion to Catholicism. The Turl is a small street near the Bodleian.

The third section of "Utopia", p. 34, quoting verses from Isaiah, is not a new translation. Apart from a minor alteration I have made, it is taken directly from The Jerusalem Bible. Other quotations from the Bible are also from this translation, and I gratefully acknowledge my debt to its translators and publishers.

"Two Chronicles," pp 36-38: These poems are closely based on "The Martyrdom of Polycarp" and notes in Early Christian Writings: The Apostolic Fathers, translated by Maxwell Staniforth, with revised translation and new editorial material by Andrew Louth (Harmondsworth: Penguin, 1987), 113-35; "St. Pionius" in The Catholic Encyclopedia; and "The Martyrdom of Pionius and his Companions" in H. Musurillo, The Acts of the Christian Martyrs (Oxford, 1972), pp. 137-167. The poems are also influenced by Cavafy and A. F. Moritz.

p. 38: Fasces: a bundle of rods symbolizing the authority of magistrates.

"St. Ignace," pp.39. St. Ignace, near Midland, Ontario, was the site of the deaths of the Jesuit missionaries Jean de Brebeuf and Gabriel Lalemant in 1649.

"Martin Royackers," pp. 40: Martin Royackers, a 41-year-old Jesuit priest from the farm town of Park Hill, Ontario, was shot at close range in Jamaica on 20 June 2001. Members of his community had earlier received death threats arising from their encouragement of a land cooperative. Although there is a great distance between my political views and Martin's, it is difficult not to honour a man who followed a difficult vocation and died bravely.

"Whaler," p.45: A crackie is a small yapping dog of mixed breed (Newfoundland dialect).

"The White Fleet," p.49: Stella Maris, meaning Star of the Sea, is a traditional title for Mary.

Over the Border:
There is a slight layering of fiction in this poem. While the various events and conversations occurred, they took place over a longer period and actually involved several trips by train and bus from 2001-3. I have altered the chronology and some settings to create a single narrative. The immediate reason for my travel was to burrow among Graham Greene's papers, most of which are owned by Boston College, the University of Texas at Austin, and Georgetown University. The book that came of my burrowing is Graham Greene: A Life in Letters (2007).

P. 64: Waleed and Wail al-Shehri and Satam al-Suqami stayed at the Park Inn on Boylston Street in the days before their hijacking of American Airways Flight 11 to Los Angeles. Another hijacker, Abdul Aziz al-Omari, may also have stayed there. See The Boston Globe (17 February 2005).

P. 67: The Canal Street doors of Union Station in Chicago are featured in the baby-carriage shoot-out in the film of The Untouchables (1987).

P. 71: The Nascar driver Dale Earnhardt died in a crash during the last lap of the Daytona 500 on 18 February 2001.

P.72: Bill Clinton was born in Hope, Arkansas, in 1946.
P. 77: Dr James Watson was a senior resident at Johns Hopkins when the novelist Thomas Wolfe was admitted suffering from tuberculosis. Julia Wolfe, who is portrayed as Eliza Gant in the novels, refused to accept the seriousness of her son's condition, and other family members accused the doctors of not telling them the truth.

P. 78: Shinnery oak is a deciduous shrub that grows in the American Southwest.

P. 78: Lady Bird Johnson (1912-2007) was still living when this section was written. She promoted the conservation of wildflowers and natural landscapes throughout the United States, but her efforts seem to have been especially successful in Texas. The Lady Bird Johnson Wildflower Center is now part of the University of Texas at Austin. See www.wildflower.org

P. 81: On 1 August 1966, Charles Whitman, a former marine, engaged in a shooting spree from the tower of the University of Texas. Many of his victims were on Guadalupe Street. Eventually shot dead by police officers, he was found to have a small tumour on his brain, but it is doubted whether that would account for his behaviour.

P 81: The Harry Ransom Center is a repository for manuscripts and rare books. It is part of the University of Texas at Austin.

Pp. 86-87: Union Station in Washington has a splendid website from which I have drawn information: www.unionstationdc.com

P. 87: The Gunlocke Room of Georgetown University's Lauinger Library is dedicated to special collections. I found myself in a strange dispute with the librarians over the use of Graham Greene's manuscripts, which was eventually resolved after the literary estate threatened legal action to ensure general access to the papers. A good account of the controversy can be found in Sarah Lyall, 'A Literary Battle That May Hang by a Comma,' *The New York Times* (16 March 2002), and in Lynn Truss's *Eats, Shoots & Leaves* (New York: Gotham Books, 2003), 101-2.

P. 87: It is not certain that Henry Kissinger originated this quip, but he certainly uses it often.

P. 87: Catherine: Graham Greene conducted a long affair with Catherine Walston, and the relationship inspired his novel The End of the Affair (1951).

P .88-89: I have drawn here on an essay by Pavel Chichikov, 'The Answer' archived at www.ncregister.com

P. 93 The World War II Memorial was opened to the public on 29 April 2004 and dedicated on 29 May.

Carmine Starnino, Editor
Michael Harris, Founding Editor

SELECTED POEMS David Solway
THE MULBERRY MEN David Solway
A SLOW LIGHT Ross Leckie
NIGHT LETTERS Bill Furey
COMPLICITY Susan Glickman
A NUN'S DIARY Ann Diamond
CAVALIER IN A ROUNDHEAD SCHOOL Errol MacDonald
VEILED COUNTRIES/LIVES Marie-Claire Blais (Translated by Michael Harris)
BLIND PAINTING Robert Melançon (Translated by Philip Stratford)
SMALL HORSES & INTIMATE BEASTS Michel Garneau
   (Translated by Robert McGee)
IN TRANSIT Michael Harris
THE FABULOUS DISGUISE OF OURSELVES Jan Conn
ASHBOURN John Reibetanz
THE POWER TO MOVE Susan Glickman
MAGELLAN'S CLOUDS Robert Allen
MODERN MARRIAGE David Solway
K. IN LOVE Don Coles
THE INVISIBLE MOON Carla Hartsfield
ALONG THE ROAD FROM EDEN George Ellenbogen
DUNINO Stephen Scobie
KINETIC MUSTACHE Arthur Clark
RUE SAINTE FAMILLE Charlotte Hussey
HENRY MOORE'S SHEEP Susan Glickman
SOUTH OF THE TUDO BEM CAFÉ Jan Conn
THE INVENTION OF HONEY Ricardo Sternberg
EVENINGS AT LOOSE ENDS Gérald Godin (Translated by Judith Cowan)
THE PROVING GROUNDS Rhea Tregebov
LITTLE BIRD Don Coles
HOMETOWN Laura Lush
FORTRESS OF CHAIRS Elisabeth Harvor
NEW & SELECTED POEMS Michael Harris
BEDROCK David Solway
TERRORIST LETTERS Ann Diamond
THE SIGNAL ANTHOLOGY Edited by Michael Harris
MURMUR OF THE STARS: SELECTED SHORTER POEMS Peter Dale Scott
WHAT DANTE DID WITH LOSS Jan Conn
MORNING WATCH John Reibetanz
JOY IS NOT MY PROFESSION Muhammad al-Maghut
   (Translated by John Asfour and Alison Burch)
WRESTLING WITH ANGELS: SELECTED POEMS Doug Beardsley
HIDE & SEEK Susan Glickman
MAPPING THE CHAOS Rhea Tregebov
FIRE NEVER SLEEPS Carla Hartsfield

THE RHINO GATE POEMS George Ellenbogen
SHADOW CABINET Richard Sanger
MAP OF DREAMS Ricardo Sternberg
THE NEW WORLD Carmine Starnino
THE LONG COLD GREEN EVENINGS OF SPRING Elisabeth Harvor
FAULT LINE Laura Lush
WHITE STONE: THE ALICE POEMS Stephanie Bolster
KEEP IT ALL Yves Boisvert (Translated by Judith Cowan)
THE GREEN ALEMBIC Louise Fabiani
THE ISLAND IN WINTER Terence Young
A TINKERS' PICNIC Peter Richardson
SARACEN ISLAND: THE POEMS OF ANDREAS KARAVIS David Solway
BEAUTIES ON MAD RIVER: SELECTED AND NEW POEMS Jan Conn
WIND AND ROOT Brent MacLaine
HISTORIES Andrew Steinmetz
ARABY Eric Ormsby
WORDS THAT WALK IN THE NIGHT Pierre Morency
   (Translated by Lissa Cowan and René Brisebois)
A PICNIC ON ICE: SELECTED POEMS Matthew Sweeney
HELIX: NEW AND SELECTED POEMS John Steffler
HERESIES: THE COMPLETE POEMS OF ANNE WILKINSON, 1924-1961
   Edited by Dean Irvine
CALLING HOME Richard Sanger
FIELDER'S CHOICE Elise Partridge
MERRYBEGOT Mary Dalton
MOUNTAIN TEA Peter Van Toorn
AN ABC OF BELLY WORK Peter Richardson
RUNNING IN PROSPECT CEMETERY Susan Glickman
MIRABEL Pierre Nepveu (Translated by Judith Cowan)
POSTSCRIPT Geoffrey Cook
STANDING WAVE Robert Allen
THERE, THERE Patrick Warner
HOW WE ALL SWIFTLY: THE FIRST SIX BOOKS Don Coles
THE NEW CANON: AN ANTHOLOGY OF CANADIAN POETRY
   Edited by Carmine Starnino
OUT TO DRY IN CAPE BRETON Anita Lahey
RED LEDGER Mary Dalton
REACHING FOR CLEAR David Solway
OX Christopher Patton
THE MECHANICAL BIRD Asa Boxer
SYMPATHY FOR THE COURIERS Peter Richardson
MORNING GOTHIC: NEW AND SELECTED POEMS George Ellenbogen
36 CORNELIAN AVENUE Christopher Wiseman
THE EMPIRE'S MISSING LINKS Walid Bitar
PENNY DREADFUL Shannon Stewart
THE STREAM EXPOSED WITH ALL ITS STONES D.G. Jones
PURE PRODUCT Jason Guriel
ANIMALS OF MY OWN KIND Harry Thurston
BOXING THE COMPASS Richard Greene

Véhicule Press